Karen Wallace

Wolves

Illustrated by Jonathan Pointer

D1464729

OXFORD
UNIVERSITY PRESS

This book belongs to

OXFORD
UNIVERSITY PRESS

Great Clarendon Street, Oxford OX2 6DP

Oxford University Press is a department of the University of Oxford.
It furthers the University's objective of excellence in research, scholarship,
and education by publishing worldwide in

Oxford New York

Athens Auckland Bangkok Bogotá Buenos Aires Calcutta
Cape Town Chennai Dar es Salaam Delhi Florence Hong Kong Istanbul
Karachi Kuala Lumpur Madrid Melbourne Mexico City Mumbai
Nairobi Paris São Paulo Singapore Taipei Tokyo Toronto Warsaw

with associated companies in Berlin Ibadan

Oxford is a registered trade mark of Oxford University Press
in the UK and in certain other countries

First published 2000

Hardback ISBN 0–19–910563–4
Paperback ISBN 0–19–910564–2

1 3 5 7 9 10 8 6 4 2

Printed and bound in Spain by Edelvives

Contents

▶ Wolf hunting grounds

Deep in a forest
a grey wolf is howling.

High on a mountain
a brown wolf is hunting.

Across a wasteland
a white wolf is running.

Wolves roam and hunt in
wild places where there are no people.

grey wolf

brown wolf

white wolf

Did you know...
Two hundred years ago there were many thousands of wolves. Now there are only a few thousand left because most of their homelands have been destroyed.

▶ The grey wolf

A wolf is resting in a meadow. His fur is grey and his eyes are yellow. When he stands, he's huge and heavy. He weighs as much as a grown-up man.

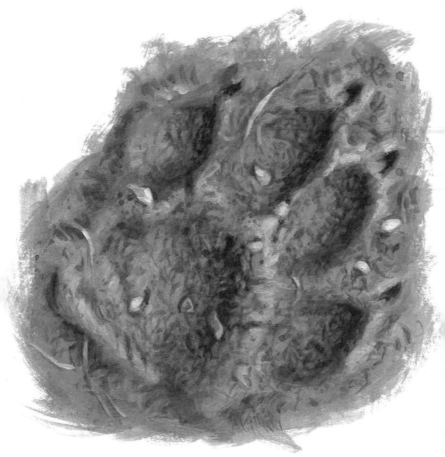

front footprint

When he walks,
his paws leave
print marks.
They're almost
as big as a
man's hand!

Did you know...
A wolf's front
footprint is bigger
than his back
footprint.

▶ Wolf pack

Six more wolves come into the meadow. They all belong to the grey wolf's pack.

A wolf pack is a family and the grey wolf leads them.

The grey wolf decides where the wolf pack hunts. The grey wolf decides when the wolf pack rests.

The grey wolf chooses a brown wolf for his mate. Only she will be a mother and have his cubs.

Did you know...
The size of a wolf pack depends on how much food it can find.

▶ Wolf cubs

In springtime, when the days are warmer, the brown wolf finds a cave and has four cubs.

They're blind and deaf and look like puppies. They suck her milk and start to grow.

A few weeks later, when the cubs have teeth, their mother chews up meat and feeds it to them.

Did you know...
Wolf cubs are born with blue eyes. They turn to yellow when they are three months old.

Wolf cubs tumble in the sunshine.
They pretend to fight.
They pretend to hunt.
They watch and learn from the
wolves around them.

Did you know...
The whole wolf pack helps to look
after the cubs.

▶ Wolf voices

A wolf pack howls for many reasons.

One howl is thin and high and lonely. That wolf is calling for a mate.

One howl is fierce. It's a warning for other wolves to keep away.

One howl is deep and strong and joyful. This grey wolf has food to feed his pack.

Did you know...
Wolves also howl to show they are happy when cubs are born.

 # Wolf signals

Wolf packs have rules they all obey.

When there's food, the grey wolf eats first. If a young wolf is hungry and crawls too near, the grey wolf shows his teeth and growls a warning.

When the young wolf whimpers and rolls on to his back, that means he's sorry and he'll wait his turn.

Wolves say different things with their faces and bodies.

I am happy.

I am angry.

I am ready.

▶ Wolf senses

The grey wolf is sitting in the meadow.

With his ears, he hears a mole in the ground.

With his nose, he smells a deer in the grass.

With his eyes, he sees a fly on a flower.

The grey wolf uses all his senses. He needs each one to stay alive.

Did you know...
Wolves have extraordinary memories. They never forget what they have seen, heard or smelt.

Wolf food

The wolf pack gathers in the meadow. They're hungry. Food is hard to find.

Their favourite food is deer and caribou, but they've only eaten mice and weasels.

The grey wolf stops. He sniffs and listens. A moose is hiding in the forest.

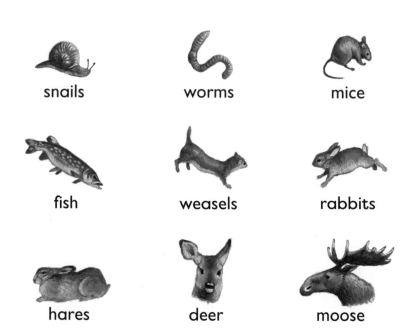

snails

worms

mice

fish

weasels

rabbits

hares

deer

moose

Did you know...
A wolf can live
without food for
two weeks or more.

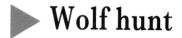 Wolf hunt

The grey wolf runs and the others follow.

A wolf pack always hunts together.

They run in line behind their leader. Their long, strong legs pound through the snow. If the leader gets tired, a new wolf takes over.

The pack chases the moose until
he falls.

The wolves attack and their
razor-sharp teeth tear up the meat.

Did you know...
A wolf's jaw is powerful enough to
break a moose's leg bone.

Wild wolf

The wolf pack is resting in
the meadow.

They've eaten the moose and
their stomachs are full.

Suddenly the grey wolf senses danger.
He sniffs the air and looks around him.
His yellow eyes are wild and wary.

The wolf gets up and the others follow.

The grey wolf leads them deep into the forest.

They run to a place where no one will find them.

▶ Glossary

This glossary will help you to understand what some important words mean. You can find them in this book by using the page numbers given below.

 caribou A caribou is a large deer-like animal. **22**

 cub A young wolf is called a cub. **12, 13, 15, 17**

 howl A howl is a long, loud, crying noise. **4, 16, 17**

 hunt To hunt means to chase and kill other animals for food. **4, 10, 15, 24**

 mate A mate is one of a pair of animals that come together to have young. **10, 16**

moose A moose is a large animal with antlers.

22, 26, 27

 pack A pack is a group of animals that live as one family.

8, 10, 11, 15–18, 22, 24, 26, 27

 roam To roam means to wander about. **4**

 senses Using our senses means being able to see, smell, hear, touch and taste things.

20, 21

Reading Together

Oxford Reds have been written by leading children's authors who have a passion for particular non-fiction subjects. So as well as up-to-date information, fascinating facts and stunning pictures, these books provide powerful writing which draws the reader into the text.

Oxford Reds are written in simple language, checked by educational advisors. There is plenty of repetition of words and phrases, and all technical words are explained. They are an ideal vehicle for helping your child develop a love of reading – by building fluency, confidence and enjoyment.

You can help your child by reading the first few pages out loud, then encourage him or her to continue alone. You could share the reading by taking turns to read a page or two. Or you could read the whole book aloud, so your child knows it well before tackling it alone.

Oxford Reds will help your child develop a love of reading and a lasting curiosity about the world we live in.

Sue Palmer
Writer and Literacy Consultant